X

TRIANGLE HISTORIES
★★★★★ ★★★★★
THE REVOLUTIONARY WAR

SAMUEL ADAMS

Kate Davis

BLACKBIRCH®
PRESS

THOMSON
GALE

San Diego • Detroit • New York • San Francisco • Cleveland
New Haven, Conn. • Waterville, Maine • London • Munich

THOMSON

GALE

For more information, contact
The Gale Group, Inc.
27500 Drake Rd.
Farmington Hills, MI 48331-3535
Or you can visit our Internet site at http://www.gale.com

Photo credits: Cover, cover (inset), pages 5, 7, 9, 27, 44, 47, 60, 62, 80, 85, 88, 92, 95 © North Wind Picture Archives; pages 10, 17, 20, 28, 31, 33, 38, 50, 59, 65,70, 99 © historypictures.com; page 18 © Archivo Iconografico, S.A./CORBIS; pages 23, 52, 86, 93 © Historical Picture Archive/ CORBIS; pages 29, 72, 75, 77 © Bettman/CORBIS; pages 40, 63, 79, 90 © Archiving Early America

LIBRARY OF CONGRESS CATALOGING-IN-PUBLICATION DATA

Davis, Kate.
  Samuel Adams / by Kate Davis.
    p. cm. — (Triangle history of the American Revolution. Revolutionary War leaders)
Includes index.
Summary: A biography of the patriot, Samuel Adams, from his religious upbringing and education to his important role in the American Revolution.
  ISBN 1-56711-612-4 (lib. bdg. : alk. paper)
  1. Adams, Samuel, 1722-1803—Juvenile literature. 2. Politicians—United States—
Biography—Juvenile literature. 3. United States. Declaration of Independence—
Signers—Biography—Juvenile literature. 4. United States—History—Revolution, 1775-
1783—Biography—Juvenile literature. [1. Adams, Samuel, 1722-1803. 2. Politicians. 3.
United States—History—Revolution, 1775-1783 .] I. Title. II. Series.
  E302.6.A2 D38 2003
  973.3'092—dc21   2002005269

Printed in China
10 9 8 7 6 5 4 3 2 1

CONTENTS

PREFACE: THE AMERICAN REVOLUTION

Today, more than two centuries after the final shots were fired, the American Revolution remains an inspiring story not only to Americans, but also to people around the world. For many citizens, the well-known battles that occurred between 1775 and 1781—such as Lexington, Trenton, Yorktown, and others—represent the essence of the Revolution. In truth, however, the formation of the United States involved much more than the battles of the Revolutionary War. The creation of our nation occurred over several decades, beginning in 1763, at the end of the French and Indian War, and continuing until 1790, when the last of the original 13 colonies ratified the Constitution.

More than 200 years later, it may be difficult to fully appreciate the courage and determination of the people who fought for, and founded, our nation. The decision to declare independence was not made easily—and it was not unanimous. Breaking away from England—the ancestral land of most colonists—was a bold and difficult move. In addition to the emotional hardship of revolt, colonists faced the greatest military and economic power in the world at the time.

The first step on the path to the Revolution was essentially a dispute over money. By 1763, England's treasury had been drained in order to pay for the French and Indian War. British lawmakers, as well as England's new ruler, King George III, felt that the colonies should help to pay for the war's expense and for the cost of housing the British troops who remained in the colonies. Thus began a series of oppressive British tax acts and other laws that angered the colonists and eventually provoked full-scale violence.

King George III

The Stamp Act of 1765 was followed by the Townshend
Acts in 1767. Gradually, colonists were forced to pay
taxes on dozens of everyday goods from playing cards to
paint to tea. At the same time, the colonists had no say in
the passage of these acts. The more colonists complained
that "taxation without representation is tyranny," the
more British lawmakers claimed the right to make laws

for the colonists "in all cases whatsoever." Soldiers and tax collectors were sent to the colonies to enforce the new laws. In addition, the colonists were forbidden to trade with any country but England.

Each act of Parliament pushed the colonies closer to unifying in opposition to English laws. Boycotts of British goods inspired protests and violence against tax collectors. Merchants who continued to trade with the Crown risked attacks by their colonial neighbors. The rising violence soon led to riots against British troops stationed in the colonies and the organized destruction of British goods. Tossing tea into Boston Harbor was just one destructive act. That event, the Boston Tea Party, led England to pass the so-called Intolerable Acts of 1774. The port of Boston was closed, more British troops were sent to the colonies, and many more legal rights for colonists were suspended.

Finally, there was no turning back. Early on an April morning in 1775, at Lexington Green in Massachusetts, the first shots of the American Revolution were fired. Even after the first battle, the idea of a war against England seemed unimaginable to all but a few radicals. Many colonists held out hope that a compromise could be reached. Except for the Battle of Bunker Hill and some minor battles at sea, the war ceased for much of 1775. During this time, delegates to the Continental Congress struggled to reach a consensus about the next step.

During those uncertain months, the Revolution was fought, not on a military battlefield, but on the battlefield of public opinion. Ardent rebels—especially Samuel Adams and Thomas Paine—worked tirelessly to keep the spirit of revolution alive. They stoked the fires of revolt by writing letters and pamphlets, speaking at public gatherings, organizing boycotts, and devising other forms of protest. It was their brave efforts that kept others focused on liberty and freedom until July 4, 1776. On that day, Thomas Jefferson's Declaration of Independence left no doubt about the intentions of the colonies. As John Adams wrote afterward, the "revolution began in hearts and minds not on the battlefield."

As unifying as Jefferson's words were, the United States did not become a nation the moment the Declaration of Independence claimed the right of all people to "life, liberty, and the pursuit of happiness." Before, during, and after the war, Americans who spoke of their "country" still generally meant whatever colony was their home. Some colonies even had their own navies during the war, and a few sent their own representatives to Europe to seek aid for their colony alone while delegates from the Continental Congress were doing the same job for the whole United States. Real national unity did not begin to take hold until the inauguration of George Washington in 1789, and did not fully bloom until the dawn of the 19th century.

The story of the American Revolution has been told for more than two centuries and may well be told for centuries to come. It is a tribute to the men and women who came together during this unique era that, to this day, people the world over find inspiration in the story of the Revolution. In the words of the Declaration of Independence, these great Americans risked "their lives, their fortunes, and their sacred honor" for freedom.

The Minuteman statue stands in Concord, Massachusetts.

Introduction:
"What a Glorious
Morning Is This!"

★ ★ ★ ★ ★

Samuel Adams heard the pounding at Reverend Jonas Clarke's front door just after midnight on April 19, 1775. A militia guard stationed inside the Clarke home angrily called to the visitor to stop making so much noise.

"Noise?" replied the rider, who Adams recognized as Paul Revere. "You'll have noise enough before long! The Regulars are coming out!"

John Hancock joined Adams at the upstairs window. They rushed down the stairs.

Once inside, Revere told the two men that the British were marching toward Lexington to arrest them. Governor Thomas Gage had sent the redcoats on the mission first to Lexington, then on to capture the gunpowder at Concord.

Adams turned to one of the guards and sent him racing to the green to ring the village bell. Within an hour, more than 130 men had assembled. Adams then had the coach prepared so that he and Hancock could leave. The two men packed hurriedly, though Hancock was not convinced they should go.

The gathered militia stood for two hours and waited for the redcoats to arrive. Finally, at 3 o'clock in the morning, Captain John Parker disbanded his men.

Hancock finally agreed to leave, just as a young teen, William Diamond, beat his drum to summon the men. Just 70 of the original militia returned—to face more than 700 rapidly approaching British regulars.

The first shots of the American Revolution were fired in Lexington early on April 19, 1775.

Dawn broke as Major John Pitcairn's redcoats marched onto Lexington Green. Parker faced his militia troops. "Stand your ground," he commanded. "If they mean to have a war, let it begin here!"

Pitcairn called out across the green. "Disperse, ye rebels, ye villains, in the name of the king!"

Parker looked at the crack British troops, and feared a massacre. He told his men to take their weapons and leave. Suddenly a shot rang out. Immediately a volley erupted. The militiamen fired off a few shots, but they were no match for the redcoats. When the British finally ceased fire, eight patriots lay dead or dying on the green.

Hancock wrung his hands in grief. Adams, however, felt a glimmer of hope. The colonials had stood up to the tyranny of British rule. "Oh! What a glorious morning is this!" he exclaimed.

9

Chapter 1

THE RELIGIOUS REBEL

Historians have called Samuel Adams a public rabble-rouser and a private failure. Many consider him the most passionate supporter for the cause of American liberty. Throughout his life, he was barely able to support his own family. He dressed in tattered clothes and worn-out shoes, and refused to wear a powdered wig in the style of the day. Yet, without the efforts of this eccentric man, there might have been no American Revolution and no United States. For that reason, Samuel Adams is known as the "Father of the American Revolution."

OPPOSITE: In the mid-1700s, Boston was one of the busiest and most important ports of the colonies.

Early Life

Samuel Adams was born to Samuel Adams, Sr., and Mary Fifield Adams on September 27, 1722, in Boston, Massachusetts. He was called Samuel, not Sam, throughout his life. His mother gave birth to twelve children in all, but only three lived to adulthood—a sister, Mary, born five years before Samuel, and a brother, Joseph, six years his junior. Such a survival rate was not unusual in the eighteenth century, before modern medicines were developed.

Samuel was a distant older cousin of John Adams, who became the second U.S. president. The two men had the same great-great-grandfather, Henry Adams, who had come to America from England in 1638.

The Adams family lived in Boston in a large house on Purchase Street. Next door was a brewery owned and operated by Samuel's father. His ancestors had brought from England the art of making barley malt for baking and brewing.

The elder Samuel Adams was relatively successful and widely respected as a wise and good man. He served as a justice of the peace, a town officer called a "selectman," and, later, as a member of the Massachusetts assembly.

Despite his political prominence, he did not agree with the royal governor's policies. Like many Massachusetts colonists, he resented the fact that England's king, who ruled from across a huge ocean, had the power to appoint the royal governor and his council, who governed the colony. These men were charged, among other duties, with enforcement of the Navigation Acts, which had been passed by Parliament in 1696. Under these laws, all trade goods that traveled between the colonies and England had to be carried in English-built ships. All European goods bound for the colonies had to come from England or pass through England to be taxed. Colonial products could be exported only to England or another British colony.

Even more infuriating to the elder Adams and many colonists was the corruption that arose from this system. Merchants commonly smuggled goods in and out of Boston and other colonial ports in the early 1700s. They got away with violating the law because they paid bribes to royal lawmakers or appointees to allow goods to pass. Thus, the wealthiest colonists were able to obtain and sell non-English goods simply by paying a bribe. Samuel's father and many other colonists hated the unfairness of this system and the power of the wealthy.

As part of his reaction against the corrupt system, Adams formed a secret workingman's group with shipmasters and shipwrights, or ship's carpenters. This "Caulkers' Club" represented poorer citizens and attempted to elect trustworthy people to local government offices, so that the common people could have at least some voice in their government.

13

Young Samuel Adams often spent hours at his father's side during meetings of the club.

Puritan Roots

Another foundation in the younger Adams's life was religion. His father was an assistant, or deacon, at the Old South Church in Boston. Samuel's mother was deeply religious and hoped that her oldest son would become a minister.

Although Samuel's commitment to democracy grew out of his father's membership in the Caulker's Club, his belief in liberty grew out of the religious teachings that ruled his upbringing. Both of Samuel's parents were descended from Puritans, the Christian sect that established the Massachusetts Bay Colony in 1630. Puritans believed in virtues such as honesty, self-reliance, frugality, and hard work. Sunday services included songs, prayer, and sermons that lasted for hours.

Samuel's father was an Independent Puritan, or Congregationalist. The members of this sect ruled their churches as a group. They elected their ministers, and believed that people were free to arrive at their own religious conclusions. Their churches also served as meetinghouses, where people from all levels of society debated not only religious concepts but ideas about how all people should be governed. Throughout Samuel's childhood, he listened as the church debates began to reflect the independent political attitudes of an increasing number of colonists.

Samuel's City

On Samuel's eighth birthday in 1730, Boston turned 100 years old. One century earlier, the town had been a small religious settlement. By 1730, Boston was a prosperous seaport city, one of the largest in the 13 colonies. From the windows of his home that overlooked the harbor, Samuel could see cargoes arrive on tall-masted sailing ships from England.

★ In 1732, George Washington was born in Virginia. ★

He loved to walk along the docks and visit with the "mechanics," as workers were called. Customers could find merchants of every kind—candle- and soapmakers, wine sellers, silversmiths, clockmakers, importers of cloth and spices, and tavernkeepers. Farmers from outlying areas rattled down cobbled lanes in horse-drawn carts to peddle fruits and vegetables. The smell of cod, salt water, and the Adams brewery filled the air. Although the Adams family was financially comfortable, the location of the brewery near the docks brought them largely in contact with working-class people rather than the wealthy residents who lived some distance from the wharves.

Boston was located on a peninsula joined to the mainland by a narrow neck. The largest building in the city was the Old South Church, where the elder Samuel Adams served as deacon and where town meetings were held when the crowd was too large for the Town House (now called the Old State

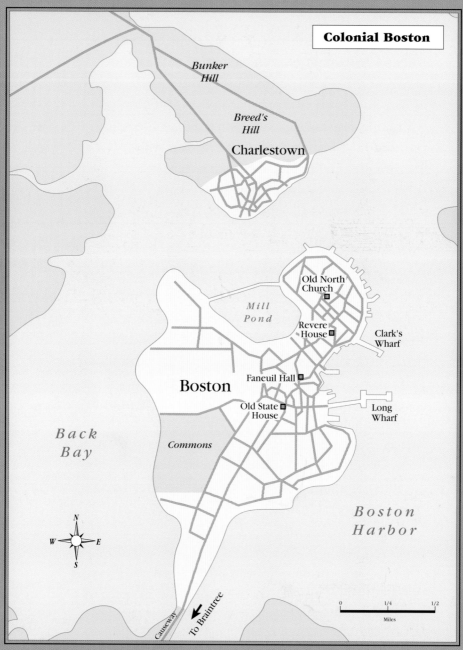

Faneuil Hall was the main marketplace in colonial Boston.

House) or Faneuil Hall, the marketplace. At the center of Boston was a park called the Common, where people strolled and farmers grazed their cows. Beacon Hill, near the Common, was the neighborhood of well-to-do families. Most inhabitants, however, were poor laborers, who struggled to earn enough money for their family's dinner each day.

Education

At a time when few adults could read or write, Samuel was fortunate to receive an education. When he was a toddler, his sister and parents taught him the alphabet and prayers. In 1728,

17

his father enrolled him in Boston Latin, the first public school in America, founded by Puritans many years earlier.

Samuel graduated from public school at the age of 13. He had studied hard and prepared for college by reading literary classics written in Latin and Greek. At graduation, he delivered a commencement speech in Latin.

When he turned 14—the usual age for attending college—Samuel entered Harvard. Like other students, he rose at 5 o'clock, attended morning prayers, ate breakfast, then had classes from 8 A.M. till noon. After a meal break, he studied from 2 P.M. until suppertime.

At Harvard, Samuel was an excellent student, seldom distracted with games or other pastimes common among young men his age. He studied science, language, philosophy, and logic. He especially favored the ideas of English philosopher John Locke, who wrote about human rights, freedom, and tolerance. Locke believed that all people ought to be equal and independent. In a perfect society, opposite opinions should be respected, and no one should have the right to harm another—not in their "life, health, liberty, or possessions."

Locke's philosophy also included another important idea—the right to protect oneself from a government that abuses its power. True political power depends on the consent of those governed, according to Locke. When a government

18

oversteps its bounds by interfering in the interests of the citizens, Locke argued, or when it rules only to benefit one class—all citizens have a right to revolt.

With his mind filled with Latin and the ideas of John Locke, Samuel graduated from college in 1740 at age 17. Despite his mother's wishes, he felt no calling to the ministry. Instead, he decided to continue at Harvard for a master's degree in classical studies. An excellent debater, Samuel first listened closely, his piercing eyes fixed on his opponent. Then he proceeded to argue his own point with great eloquence and emotion.

John Locke was a popular philosopher and political writer.

At the master's graduation ceremony in 1743, Samuel delivered a speech in Latin that raised many eyebrows. He posed the question, "Is it lawful to resist the government if the welfare of the republic is involved?" Then he answered "yes." The governor of Massachusetts, William Shirley, and his council were seated in the audience. While these royal appointees listened to the bold speaker, Adams championed the right to revolt against injustice and corrupt governments. Although those beliefs formed the foundation of Samuel's political life, he was careful to speak in general terms, without mentioning the colonies' present circumstances.

19

Chapter 2

FROM FAILURE
TO REVOLT

Samuel Adams's choice of topic for his Harvard graduation speech was motivated by more than schoolbook philosophy. During his final year in the master's program, he had witnessed his father suffer a harsh financial setback at the hands of the British government and its servants in the colonial government. During occasional visits home from college during that final year, young Adams overheard heated discussions in his father's parlor about that injustice.

OPPOSITE: The Liberty Tree in Boston was a place for colonists who opposed British taxes to gather and protest.

The Land Bank

In the 1740s, most Massachusetts colonists had little cash. Gold, silver, and copper were not mined in the colonies, and the metals were difficult to obtain from overseas. The colonists had manufactured some coins in the 1600s, but the king of England and the British Parliament forced them to stop. The Crown and the wealthiest merchants wanted only British money to be used in the colonies.

In response to the problem of a money shortage, Adams's father decided to create a bank with some friends in order to print new money. Because the value of the money was backed with their own homes and land rather than precious metals, the founders called it the "Land Bank."

Land Bank money was welcomed by many farmers and poorer citizens, but the governor felt that the new money would cause British money to decrease in value. That would be against the governor's interests because most British currency was in the hands of his wealthy friends and the merchants who traded in British goods, or those who smuggled goods and offered bribes.

In the early 1740s, a wealthy merchant, Thomas Hutchinson, was a local selectman. Like those of his class, he disliked the financial organization headed by the elder Adams. Hutchinson and his supporters began to publish newspaper stories that falsely claimed Adams was cheating the people.

22

Colonial money was engraved by craftsmen, such as Paul Revere, and printed by printers, such as Benjamin Franklin.

When the public refused to accept the stories, Hutchinson wrote to the British Parliament. In 1742, Parliament forced the Land Bank to close.

With his money now worthless, Adams fell deeply into debt. Government officials threatened to seize his home to pay back the debt. Other issues distracted them from their claim—for the time being. Hutchinson, however, did not forget the debts of Land Bank. For young Samuel Adams, his father's failure at the hands of wealthy merchants sharpened his lifelong bitterness toward the British government and its colonial officials.

23

In and Out of Jobs

When Samuel Adams completed his studies at Harvard, he was 21 and in search of an occupation. On the advice of his father, who noted his son's keen ability to win arguments, Adams began to study law. He quickly found the legal profession distasteful. For one thing, the occupation was not well respected. For another, his mother reminded him, lawyers often cared more about winning money than achieving justice.

The elder Adams turned to his friends for help in finding a job for his son. He asked his friend Thomas Cushing Sr., who ran a countinghouse, or accounting business, to hire young Samuel. Adams worked as a clerk at Cushing's firm for only a few months. He found it too hard to attend to a ledger book when there were interesting conversations on the docks and in the taverns. Whenever he had the opportunity, he discussed the political powerlessness of the average colonist with shipwrights and other working men.

Adams offered his son another chance. He loaned him about 1,000 pounds, a huge amount of money at the time, to start any business he wanted. Unskilled in practical matters, Adams immediately loaned half of the money to a troubled friend who never repaid it. Before long, the other half was gone too, and there was nothing to show for it.

For all his education, Adams did not know how to manage money. It was also true that, in some ways, money represented to him everything that was wrong with Boston. The wealthy merchants who controlled the town cared little about the poor. Adams felt it was better to live like the common man in "honorable poverty" than to succeed in business. He dressed in worn-out clothes even when his parents gave him new ones.

The elder Adams, however, would not let his son fail. He gave Adams one last opportunity—a job in his brewery, with a regular paycheck. With this newfound security, Adams started a society for political debate, called the Whipping-Post Club, because its members tongue-lashed the government.

★

In 1747, John Paul Jones was born in southern Scotland.

★

In 1747, club members began to print their own newspaper, the *Public Advertiser*. Adams honed his writing skills in articles for the paper that defended workers' rights. He was finally doing what he loved as he discussed politics, wrote, and championed civil liberties.

Family Tragedies

One year later, in March 1748, Adams's father died. The house on Purchase Street and the family brewery passed into his son's hands. Now that he had a home and a business, he felt for the first time that he might consider marriage. He began to court Elizabeth Checkley, the daughter of the minister who conducted his father's funeral.

A year later, Adams's mother died. After a period of mourning, Samuel Adams and Elizabeth Checkley were married in October 1749. They

25

settled into the Adams home and began a family. Three of their children died before the age of three months. Two survived: Samuel, born in 1751, and Hannah, born in 1756.

During the early years of his marriage, Adams became active in town government. He served on a volunteer committee to evaluate schools, which often took him away from overseeing the family brewery.

The year Hannah was born, Adams was elected the town tax collector, a one-year paid position. His job was to collect the taxes owed by residents. Failure to do so meant he would be responsible for the debts.

True to his roots as a supporter of the working class and to his membership in the Whipping-Post Club, Adams felt sorry for the people who owed taxes and could not pay them. He soon became a failure at this job. The brewery was also going downhill, as customer after customer chose brewers whose beer tasted better.

His greatest loss, however, came in 1757, when Adams's wife died shortly after delivering a still-born son. Within nine years, Adams had lost both parents, four children, and his wife. He now had two small children to raise on his own.

Problems with the Governor's Man

While Adams was preoccupied with personal hardship, the British army was busy on the western frontier of the colonies, engaged in a fight to keep

British troops fought French troops and their Native American allies in the French and Indian War.

the French from taking control of territories in the Ohio River Valley. Many colonists, including George Washington, helped the British fight against the French in North America. This war was called the French and Indian War in America. In Europe,

27

the war involved other European nations who, like the British and French, were struggling to make their empires larger. The Europeans called the war the Seven Years' War. To win, the British needed more than manpower. The war was costly, and the governor of Massachusetts was under pressure to raise funds any way he could.

Thomas Hutchinson became Adams's bitter enemy.

In 1758, Thomas Hutchinson was appointed the lieutenant governor of Massachusetts. It was a good time to settle his old score, and he sent the county sheriff to Adams's home to collect Adams's Land Bank debt. There, the sheriff posted a notice that the Adams estate and brewery would be auctioned off.

Adams was enraged. The house and business were all he had left of his inheritance. He vowed to sue the sheriff if he tried to seize the house. He wrote letters to the newspaper. Finally, the sheriff dropped the sale.

Meanwhile, Adams's own debts continued to mount. By 1764, he owed more than 8,000 pounds in uncollected taxes from townsfolk. The people were so appreciative that they re-elected him tax collector.

Slavery and Samuel Adams

★ ★ ★ ★ ★

Although many people associate slavery with the large plantations of the southern colonies, slavery existed legally in every colony until the late 1700s. In 1722, when Adams was born, African

> TO Be fold, — a likely Negro Wench, about 37 Years of Age, fit for all forts of House Work, and is a tolerable good Cook; she can be well recommended, mII
>
> TO BE SOLD,
>
> A LIKELY young fturdy Negro Wench, about 19 years of Age, fit for Town or Country; She is a trufty Wench, and, with a little Inftruction, being young, may be of great fervice to any Family in Town. Enquire of Weyman, in Broad-Street.

Ads in colonial papers offered African Americans for sale.

American slaves made up about 10 percent of Boston's population of 16,000. In the 1760s, New York City had the second-largest urban slave population in the colonies after Charleston, South Carolina.

Most slaves in the northeast were owned by ministers, doctors, and merchants. Adams's second wife, Betsy, the daughter of a merchant, received a slave girl, named Surry, as a gift from her father shortly before she married Adams. Adams had strong objections to slavery. Before their wedding, he told Betsy that "a slave cannot live in my house. If she comes, she must be free." After their marriage, Adams filled out the papers to give Surry her freedom. Surry was so grateful to be free that she asked to remain with the Adamses and work for them.

Surry lived with the Adamses, kept house, and cooked for nearly 50 years. She became a part of the family, and was said to have dumped pots of food on visitors to the home who disagreed with Adams on political issues.

After his re-election, Adams married for a second time. Elizabeth Wells, his new wife, was the daughter of a close friend of his father's. Because Samuel did not want to call his new wife by the same name as his first wife, she became Betsy Adams. Adams then began to make his name one of the most famous—or infamous—in the colonies.

The Stamp Act

In 1763, the Treaty of Paris ended the French and Indian War. Early the next April, the colonies learned that England expected them to pay the British war debt and the cost of maintaining a small standing army in America. England's Parliament passed a tax known as the Stamp Act. This law, which was scheduled to take effect in November 1765, required colonists to buy stamps bearing the royal coat of arms and place them on all papers and legal documents—wills, deeds, birth certificates, marriage licenses, bills of sale, diplomas, even playing cards and newspapers.

To Adams, who had grown up with a dislike of British control, this was just the latest abuse of power the colonists had suffered. He had spoken out against British injustice for years. Yet because much of the abuse of the Navigation Acts was carried on by wealthy men behind closed doors, few colonists were aware of the way in which they were cheated. Adams had difficulty making his fellow colonists aware of the ways in which the British government took advantage of them.

Sugarcane, grown in the West Indies by African slaves, played a vital role in England's economy.

When the war ended, Adams and others watched the oppression of the colonists grow more direct and intense. Under "writs of assistance," British customs agents searched buildings and ships without warrants (permission of the courts). In 1764, two additions to the Navigation Acts, the Sugar Act and the Currency Act, forced colonists to buy sugar only from British colonies in the West Indies and pay for it only with British money. The latest offense, the Stamp Act, now took money directly from business transactions.

During the summer of 1765, Adams's friend, lawyer James Otis, spoke out numerous times against the Stamp Act. He argued in his speeches that because the colonists had no seat or voice in the British Parliament, they had no vote on the issue of taxes. His speeches included the famous phrase that spread throughout the colonies: "Taxation without representation is tyranny!"

Once he realized that the Stamp Act had a more direct effect on the average colonists than the

31

Navigation Acts, Adams saw an opportunity to create widespread resistance to the Crown. To fan the flames of outrage, he went door to door throughout Boston and explained how much the tax stamps intruded into the life of every colonist. No one who married, had children, read newspapers, or conducted business would be immune from purchasing stamps.

Adams felt that to abolish the tax would require opposition on many fronts. He began a propaganda campaign. He wrote pamphlets against the Stamp Act and sent letters to newspapers, sometimes under pen names. His work appeared in many papers, including the *Boston Gazette*, which was read by thousands of colonists. Each issue carried a few political essays, many composed by Adams.

In his writing, Adams claimed that British taxes on the colonies took away the colonists' freedom. He also pointed out that the salaries of colonial officials, who were supposed to oversee the public good, were paid with royal funds. This made the officials more likely to do the king's bidding, whether it benefited the colonists or not. In other words, the taxes that came from the colonists went into the pockets of royal officials, who did nothing for the colonies but take more taxes. It was governmental robbery, Adams argued.

Adams drafted formal documents to protest the taxation of the colonies and gave them to royal councils. "If our trade may be taxed, why not our lands? Why not the produce of our lands, and

affix the STAMP.

This is the Place to

Colonial newspapers printed protests such as this one against the hated Stamp Act.

every thing we possess, or use?" he wrote. "We are reduced from . . . free subjects, to the state of tributary slaves."

Adams called upon the other colonies to unite in opposition to the taxes. In fact, Massachusetts was not the only colony that had strong feelings against the Stamp Act. In Virginia, Patrick Henry was defiant. In an address to the House of Burgesses, the colony's legislature, Henry carefully affirmed his allegiance to the king, but he also pledged loyalty to "his Country's Dying liberty." His Virginia Resolves, which protested the Stamp Act, were adopted. In Pennsylvania, the assembly also adopted resolutions that denounced the act.

For the protests to have greater effect, Adams felt that the colonies should speak with a more unified voice. He suggested the establishment of a system of communication up and down the coast for that purpose, and he wrote to leaders in other colonies about unifying the colonists against the Stamp Act.

For the first time in his life, Adams felt he was doing meaningful work. He became a well-known figure on the streets of Boston. He was known as "The Man of the Town Meeting" because he spoke at every public gathering.

Sons of Liberty

By the summer of 1765, in popular gathering places such as taverns and meetinghouses, discussions grew heated over the Stamp Act. Citizens banded together and vowed to resist the taxation. One group of tradesmen, printers, merchants, and artisans, who called themselves the Loyal Nine, met in secret to plan defiant actions.

Similar groups formed throughout the colonies. Many colonists were encouraged by the fact that a man named Isaac Barré, a member of Parliament, had spoken out against the Stamp Act. He had predicted outrage from the colonists, whom he called "these Sons of Liberty." The name had a patriotic appeal, and groups of Americans soon adopted it for their organizations. Sons of Liberty chapters formed first in Massachusetts and New York City, then throughout New England, the Carolinas, and Virginia. American political activism was born.

In Boston, at work behind the scenes to avoid arrest for treason, Adams enlisted dockworkers, fishermen, farmers, and laborers to the cause. From his days as a graduate student through his twenties and thirties, Adams had always spoken out on and written about issues that affected the average colonist. Thus, these working men, who respected Adams for his strong opinions, were more than willing to lend their muscle to the cause of liberty.

Under the Liberty Tree

On the night of August 14, 1765, in Boston, members of the Sons of Liberty met beneath a giant 120-year-old elm, which they called the "Liberty Tree." The Sons hung from the tree a dummy in the likeness of Andrew Oliver, the tax-stamp distributor, who was also the brother-in-law of Thomas Hutchinson. A boot with a devil sticking out of it was suspended by a rope from another branch. The message was that the stamp officer was in league with the devil. Since these activities were illegal, Adams kept his distance from public protests, but most Sons acknowledged him as the leader of the group.

The day after the protest at the Liberty Tree, the governor ordered Boston sheriffs to remove the dummies. They refused because they were too frightened of the Sons of Liberty to do so. Later that evening, as crowds looked on, the Sons cut down the figures and marched through the streets with them, shouting "Liberty, property, and no stamps!"

The mob proceeded to the docks and smashed a hut that Oliver had built to store and sell the tax stamps. Then they paraded to his home, where rowdy men broke his windows, axed his door, and smashed his furniture. Others beheaded the dummy, set fire to it, and used planks from the stamp hut to fuel a roaring bonfire. Alarmed by the angry crowd, Oliver came out on his balcony and promised to resign from his post.

The Sons of Liberty were emboldened by their success. Twelve days later, mobs marched to Hutchinson's mansion and vandalized it. They stole his money and silver, then threw his books, papers, and furniture into the street and set a roaring fire with them.

These street protests became known as the Stamp Act riots. Although Adams organized the Sons of Liberty, it is not known whether he supported the violence. Some people objected to the unruly mobs, but many were glad that the Sons of Liberty were taking a stand against the British. They welcomed Adams's determination in particular. In September 1765, he decided to run for public office and was elected to a seat on the legislature.

The Protests Spread

During the fall of 1765, as the deadline for the Stamp Act to take effect approached, word spread that other colonies had resorted to riots. The Sons of Liberty in New York had burned the stamp paper, reduced their governor's coach to ashes, and vandalized his home. Similar protests took place in New Jersey and Connecticut.

The widespread dislike of Parliament's act convinced many colonists that the time was right to unite and take the action a step further. Adams joined with James Otis to call for a Stamp Act Congress to develop a plan for the repeal of the stamp tax. Delegates from nine colonies attended the convention in New York City in October 1765.

When the Stamp Act took effect in November, many colonial merchants and printers tried to ignore it. Boston closed its courts to business rather than put stamps on official documents. Other cities did the same. With few troops in America, the British Crown could not enforce the tax.

Finally in February 1766, Parliament repealed the Stamp Act. Boston celebrated with church bells, fireworks, and parades. Colonists even applauded the king of England.

Adams, however, thought that the colonists' problems with the British were far from over. A few wealthy men loyal to the Crown were still in positions of power, and Adams believed the colonies would remain controlled by corrupt appointees of King George III. The only way to avoid this, he felt, was for colonists to obtain a voice in their government.

With the repeal of the Stamp Act, Adams was concerned that the protests would come to a standstill. He wanted the agitation for change to continue to build. The street resistance had given voice to the injustice the colonists felt, but lasting freedom would require the colonists to increase their opposition to British control.

Chapter 3

THE ROAD TO REVOLUTION

Because of his efforts to get the Stamp Act repealed, colonists now regarded Adams as a political leader. The British Crown, on the other hand, considered him a thorn in its side. Men in England urged Massachusetts lieutenant governor Thomas Hutchinson to bribe Adams with gifts or a royal office to cease his written and organized protests. Adams refused all offers, and Hutchinson called him "obstinate and inflexible."

OPPOSITE: A tax collector is tarred and feathered in a political cartoon.

Adams's cousin John, on the other hand, described him as a man of "steadfast integrity," a "universal good character." The cousins had gotten to know each other better when John began to work as a lawyer in Boston. They had found themselves on the same side of the taxation issue. John said his cousin had "the most thorough understanding of liberty" and was "zealous and keen in the cause."

As a leader, Adams soon began to ally himself with other prominent men of Boston—Dr. Joseph Warren, his family physician; Josiah Quincy, a lawyer; and, especially, John Hancock. Hancock was one of the wealthiest merchants in New England. In contrast to Adams, who often wore a tattered red coat, Hancock dressed at the height of fashion, traveled in a fancy carriage, and held lavish parties. A Harvard

John Hancock (picured) was Adams's lifelong friend.

Samuel Adams

graduate, he was drawn to intelligent men and believed Adams to be a political genius.

At the age of 27, Hancock had received a huge inheritance from the uncle who raised him. His uncle had acquired a great deal of his fortune in the early 1700s by smuggling goods into Boston and New York from abroad in violation of the Navigation Acts. Hancock himself continued to skirt the law by smuggling.

With the repeal of the Stamp Act, Adams had toned down the actions of the Sons of Liberty and reorganized them into a political party called the Liberty Party. Because many critics accused the new Liberty Party of being filled with unruly hooligans, Adams felt that enlisting influential men to the popular cause might build respect. In 1766, the party nominated Hancock to be the Boston representative to the Massachusetts legislature, and he was elected handily.

Like Adams, Hancock cared about the protection of colonial rights. As public support for those rights grew, Adams set his sights on something far greater than the marches that had led to the Stamp Act riots. He believed the colonies should have more control over their future and be less dependent on their "mother country," England, which had its own social and political problems. Adams had a vision of a new "mighty empire" in the colonies. The citizens would be virtuous, the children educated, and justice would be the rule. Public offices would not be filled with wealthy appointees but with men

41

of integrity, who served the community, instead of a distant royal court.

Townshend Acts

The repeal of the Stamp Act gave many colonists hope that England had changed its policies toward America. That hope faded when Parliament passed the Declaratory Act. It stated that the British had the right to enact laws for the colonies "in all cases whatsoever."

Less than a year later, British chancellor Charles Townshend called for everyday items, such as glass, paint, paper, lead, and tea, to be taxed as they arrived in American ports. Parliament cooperated and passed these taxes under the Townshend Acts.

Once again, the Sons of Liberty gathered beneath the Liberty Tree. Adams encouraged citizens to boycott British products. Protesters took to the streets again, and vandals broke windows of merchants who sold British goods. Those who did not heed the warnings were coated with hot tar and feathers, a cruel and painful practice.

Adams enthusiastically planned protests against the royal governor and those who profited from the new taxes. He wrote new letters to the newspapers and contacted other colonists to ask them to unite in a demand for American rights. In February 1768, he drafted the Massachusetts Circular Letter for the state House of Representatives, in which he attacked the British practice of taxation without representation.

Adams's constant taunts of the royal government and his appeals to his fellow colonists to protest enraged royal governor Francis Bernard. He called Adams "the most dangerous man in Massachusetts, a man dedicated to . . . mischief."

In response to Adams and the new protests, Bernard decided to get tough on customs inspectors who allowed smuggled goods into Boston. In June, he ordered British officers to seize John Hancock's ship *Liberty* to punish him for smuggling and refusing to pay import duties. Hundreds of angry longshoremen, who unloaded boats, and other Hancock supporters retaliated by burning a boat that belonged to the British customs officer.

★

In 1768, tax collector Thomas Paine joined the Headstrong Club in England to argue political issues.

★

The Crown decided to send troops into Boston to enforce the Townshend Acts and assert its hold over the colonists. In October 1768, about 700 British soldiers marched off troop ships into Boston. Before long, even more ships arrived, until a total of 4,000 troops—two regiments in all— filled the city. The army's presence only encouraged more support for the efforts of Adams and others, and did nothing to pacify the city.

The redcoats needed housing, but anyone who offered to shelter them risked punishment from the Sons of Liberty. Even Loyalists, those who supported the king, were unwilling to put themselves at peril. The troops resorted to camping out on Boston Common. They took over Fanueil Hall and, in an attempt to bully the colonists,

43

The arrival of British troops in Boston created a mood of rebellion among colonists.

Samuel Adams

aimed cannons at the State House, where the Massachusetts legislature met.

Many colonists, including Adams, refused to be intimidated. He urged townspeople to harass the troops. Youngsters taunted the red-coated soldiers with the epithet "lobsterbacks." They tossed eggs and insults at them. Adams even encouraged his pet dog to nip at passing soldiers.

Adams also started a propaganda campaign in the summer of 1768, one that was more extreme than the one he organized to protest the Stamp Act. This time, instead of reasoned articles, he planted exaggerated news stories under a pen name. These stories accused the troops of beating citizens and worse. Adams believed that he had achieved a degree of success when the governor was recalled to England to answer charges that the redcoats had abused Boston residents, but the triumph was tempered by the fact that Bernard's successor was none other than Adams's archenemy, Thomas Hutchinson.

Bloodshed in the Streets

In 1770, the situation in Boston went from bad to worse. One night, two young boys posted signs in front of a merchant's shop that mocked him for dealing in British goods. The Loyalist businessman was so angry that he shot at the boys. One of them, 12-year-old Christopher Snider, soon died from his wounds. Hundreds of mourners turned out for his funeral. They seized the merchant and

45

insisted that he be imprisoned and tried for murder. He was convicted and served a short term, but Hutchinson released him.

In March 1770, one of the key events that led to the Revolution occurred. The British soldiers in Boston were paid so poorly that they often took part-time jobs when they were off duty. This practice stole employment from American laborers. Indignant colonial workers taunted the soldiers, threw stones at them, and ganged up on them. The soldiers, who had been ordered to avoid violence as much as possible, often shoved and beat the colonists in return.

On the night of March 5, a crowd of men and boys threw rocks and snowballs at a British guard and taunted him. When the guard called for help, his captain arrived with armed soldiers.

Tempers were short. The colonists were still angry about the death of Christopher Snider as well as the fact that redcoats took their jobs. Some British troops still smarted from a recent gang beating of one of their ranks. Soon a large group of colonials pressed closely against a smaller squad of redcoats.

An officer may have yelled, "Do not FIRE!" In the noise, the soldiers claimed to have heard only "FIRE!"—and they started to shoot. In moments, 11 Bostonians had fallen, and 5 died.

The next morning, horrified citizens held a town meeting. They voted to send Adams and a committee to the State House to demand the withdrawal of the troops. At the State House, Hutchinson said he did not have the authority to do any more than remove the regiment that was responsible.

Adams was furious. "If you have the power to remove one regiment," he retorted, "you have power to remove both." Then he warned the governor that an angry crowd was ready to march to the State House unless the troops were removed. "It is at your peril if you refuse," he said. "Three thousand people...have become impatient. The whole country is in motion. Night is approaching.... Both regiments or none!"

Adams kept the outrage at a fever pitch. He called the killings a "bloody butchery." He had his friend Paul Revere create and publish a drawing that made the incident look like cold-blooded murder, with British soldiers firing point-blank at the crowd.

Hutchinson realized that he could not stand against an entire city. The thought of thousands of angry citizens descending on him persuaded him to give in. He agreed to remove both regiments, and within days, the redcoats marched back down to the wharves to embark for England on ships.

By coincidence, Parliament had repealed the Townshend Acts on the day of the bloody episode that became known as the Boston Massacre. The only offensive tax was the one that remained on tea. Bostonians considered themselves victorious, and many hoped to put the unpleasant events of the preceding years behind them.

47

The Boston Massacre enraged
colonists from New Hampshire
to Georgia.

A Watchdog for Liberty

For the next three years, relations between Massachusetts colonists and the British lawmakers remained peaceful. In late 1770, the boycott of British goods ended, and Adams fell "out of fashion," as he told his daughter. Still, he remained vigilant of the British. His motto was, "Where there is a spark of patriotic fire, we will enkindle it!" With Dr. Joseph Warren, he established a network to keep informed of events in other colonies.

In 1772, Adams, Warren, and other Bostonian Patriots—colonists who supported independence from England—formalized a Committee of Correspondence in Boston to communicate with other towns in Massachusetts. Eventually almost every colony had a committee to exchange information with other colonies about British actions in America. In 1772, there were committees in Massachusetts. In March 1773, one formed in Virginia. Within a year, every colony but Pennsylvania had a committee. They sent their messages by way of ships or fast horseback riders. This established a communication network throughout the colonies, in case rebellion was again required.

Though the protests had ceased in Boston, Hutchinson still considered Adams a troublemaker, and he was especially concerned about the committees that has been formed under Adams's direction.

Benjamin Franklin was in England when the Hutchinson letters were sent.

In 1772, Hutchinson wrote several letters to the English government in which he asked for tougher policies against the colonies and requested that troops once again be sent to America to enforce laws.

As it happened, the letters not only reached the Crown, they also reached the well-known inventor and writer Benjamin Franklin, who was in London as a business representative for the colonists.

Samuel Adams

Franklin informed colleagues in Boston about the contents of Hutchinson's letters. Although the letters were supposed to remain secret, they appeared in the *Boston Gazette* in 1773. Many citizens who had been unconcerned about the royal presence in Boston were once again outraged by the letters. Those who had been content to accept the tax on tea began to believe that it was only a matter of time before the colonists' powerlessness was reinforced by the return of the hated redcoats. Adams, who had been a forgotten man over the prior three years, was suddenly back in fashion. He was ready to channel the outrage into action.

Chapter 4

THE BRITISH
ARE COMING

In 1773, Adams directed one of the most dramatic events of public resistance in American history. Though he never claimed responsibility for it—or denied it—historians credit him as the mastermind behind the notorious uprising that became known as the Boston Tea Party.

Colonists drank tea in tremendous quantities. In order to have it, some people were willing to pay the tax on English tea, which had been left in place when the Townshend Acts were repealed. Most people, however, bought smuggled tea from Holland to get around the tax. In spring 1773, the British government was determined to change that.

OPPOSITE: The Boston Tea Party was allegedly conceived by Adams and carried out by the Sons of Liberty.

53

The Boston Tea Party came about because the British East India Company had an oversupply of tea to sell, but did not have the money to pay the import taxes in England. Parliament wanted to help the company and make money for its treasury as well. British lawmakers decided to let the company sell the tea to the American colonists without paying any duty. The money would be made up by modest tea taxes that the colonists paid. The colonists would benefit, according to British reasoning, because the cost of the tea—even with taxes—would be lower than the tea they smuggled in illegally.

Most colonists did not see it that way at all. To have tea forced on them was one more example of how they lacked a voice in their own affairs. They did not want any tax, no matter how small, to be used to fund the English government. Up and down the East Coast, colonists mounted a new campaign to boycott tea. Many switched to coffee. Others raised their own herbs for home-grown brews called "liberty tea." The boycott was so effective that sales of tea dropped by more than two-thirds.

In addition to boycotting British tea, Bostonians held town meetings, staged protests, and wrote letters to the newspapers. Adams urged his friends to "rise and resist this and every other plan laid for our destruction, as becomes wise freemen."

Under a pen name, he published an article in the *Boston Gazette* in September that described his

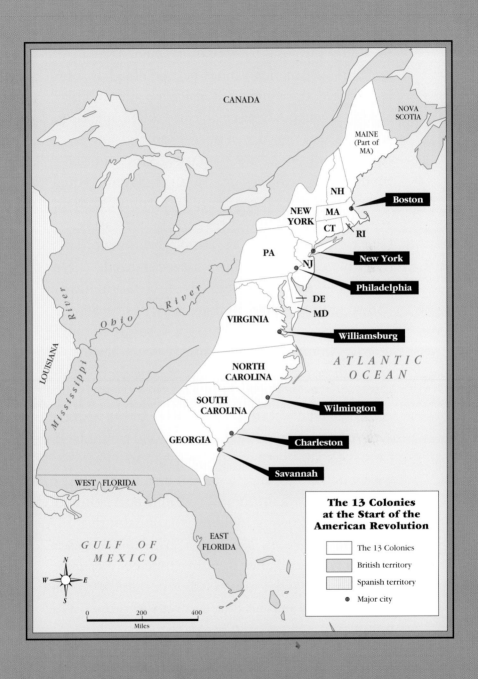

CANADA

NOVA SCOTIA

MAINE (Part of MA)

NH

NEW YORK

MA

CT

RI

Boston

PA

NJ

New York

Philadelphia

DE

MD

VIRGINIA

Williamsburg

ATLANTIC OCEAN

NORTH CAROLINA

SOUTH CAROLINA

Wilmington

GEORGIA

Charleston

Savannah

Ohio River

Mississippi River

LOUISIANA

WEST FLORIDA

EAST FLORIDA

GULF OF MEXICO

The 13 Colonies at the Start of the American Revolution

The 13 Colonies

British territory

Spanish territory

● Major city

N W E S

0   200   400
Miles

vision for a new union of states: "I beg leave to offer a proposal to my countrymen. That a congress of American states be assembled as soon as possible, draw up a Bill of Rights and publish it to the world. . . . So sensible are the people of America that they are in possession of a fine country and superior advantages . . . it cannot be thought they will ever give up their claim to equal liberty with any other people on earth; but rather, as they find their power perpetually increasing, look for [more] just liberty and government than other nations, or even Britain ever enjoyed. . . . No people that ever trod the stage of the world have had so glorious a prospect as now rises before the Americans—there is nothing good, or great, but their wisdom may acquire; and to what heights they will arrive in the progress of time no one can conceive."

Adams went on to scold England for its imperial actions, and warned that such actions would be the cause of a split between the two nations. His words were intended to turn sentiment against the British. "That Great Britain should continue to insult and alienate the growing millions who inhabit this country," he wrote, "on whom she greatly depends, and on whose alliance in future time her existence as a nation may be suspended, is perhaps as glaring an instance of human folly as ever disgraced politicians."

To Adams, a small tax was as bad as a large one, for it was the principle that mattered. Growing numbers of citizens came to agree with Adams—any taxation without representation was intolerable.

Parliament was determined to force the issue. In November, it sent three vessels loaded with tea to Boston, protected by armed ships. In response, the Sons of Liberty called for the tea agents to resign. They told the governor they would not let the ships unload their cargo. Hutchinson refused to send the ships back.

On December 16, 1773, more than 5,000 angry people assembled in the Old South Meeting House. While some gave rousing speeches, a committee proceeded to the governor's office to demand that the tea cargo ships return to England. Hutchinson promised a reply by evening, but then slipped out of town to his country house.

At the meetinghouse, Adams stood up and declared, "This meeting can do nothing more to save the country!" At those words, nearly 100 men painted their faces with coal dust and put feathers in their hair to disguise themselves as Indians. They brandished hatchets and whooped loudly as they paraded to Griffin's Wharf. Many chanted, "T(ea) is for tyranny!" Others cried, "Let every man do his duty, and be true to his country!"

> ★
> In 1773, General Charles Cornwallis was the vice treasurer of Ireland and was stationed in the Irish city of Cork.
> ★

In three groups, they rowed out to the ships. Weapons raised, the men demanded the cargo hatch keys from the captains and broke into the holds. One by one, they smashed open crates of

57

tea, 342 in all, and dumped them into the water. The armed ships never fired at them. The next morning, any crates that surfaced and could be salvaged were beaten and the contents stirred into the bay to make more "saltwater tea."

Word of the Boston Tea Party soon spread to the other colonies. New York and Maryland patriots followed with similar events.

Intolerable Laws

Before the Boston Tea Party, major protests by colonists caused Parliament to back away from its tax laws. The Boston Tea Party, however, drew a swift and tough response from Parliament and George III. British leaders insisted that the city of Boston pay for the tea, and in a series of laws that the colonists called the Intolerable Acts, the British closed the port of Boston. The acts no longer allowed towns to hold meetings to settle local matters. They declared that colonial officials accused of crimes had to be tried in England. A new Quartering Act forced Boston residents to house and feed British troops.

Finally, England replaced Hutchinson as governor with General Thomas Gage, a military leader, and prepared to send 5,000 troops to Boston to support him. Colonists were stunned. Their economy would soon be crippled, they realized, and jobs would be lost.

Adams and the colonists learned the extent of these acts in early May 1774. The Boston

Committee of Correspondence sent letters to the other colonies to report that the port would be closed and residents would have to pay for the tea that was destroyed. Most colonists supported Boston and agreed that they should not pay for the tea. Colonial committees offered to aid Massachusetts by opening their ports to Boston-bound ships and sending supplies overland.

Lieutenant General Thomas Gage had fought alongside Washington in the French and Indian War.

Gage arrived in mid-May, with his redcoats close behind. Immediately, the resistance began to rise in the city. Once again there were dangerous clashes in the streets.

Many colonists suspected that Gage would use his military muscle to round up the leaders of the rebellion—especially Adams and Hancock. Patriots put bars across the doors and windows of Adams's house to prevent British troops from breaking in.

Gage decided not to arrest Adams directly. Instead, he resorted to his predecessor's tactic. He proposed that if Adams ceased his opposition to the royal government, he could have "any benefit he should demand." Adams was also sternly

Laws allowed British soldiers to search colonists' homes for any reason.

reminded that the governor could send him to England and try him for treason.

Steadfast in his beliefs, Adams replied to Gage's aide: "Go tell Governor Gage that my peace has long since been made with the King of kings, and that it is the advice of Samuel Adams to him, no longer to insult the feelings of an already exasperated people."

The First Continental Congress

Gage had moved the Massachusetts legislature north, to Salem, where he thought there might be less agitation from Adams and his band of

Samuel Adams

"radicals," but he underestimated the number of lawmakers who supported Adams. On June 17, 1774, Adams made a secret motion in the Massachusetts house to send five delegates to the colony-wide Continental Congress in Philadelphia. When the tally was taken, only 11 men voted against it—all Loyalists. The other 120 men voted in favor of naming a delegation to the congress.

During the proceedings, one man pretended to be sick and left to alert the governor about what was taking place. Gage tried to disband the house session, but the legislators kept the doors locked until their business was completed. When they reopened, five men had been chosen to go to Philadelphia. Adams was one of the five. His commitment to the cause of liberty made him a clear choice to speak for his people.

Unlike the other men, who included his cousin John and his friend Hancock, Adams certainly did not look like a delegate. His clothes were tattered, his hair was scraggly, and his shoes were worn out. This was remedied when a new wig, hat, cane, a red coat, shoes with silver buckles, and a purse full of coins arrived at his home. Some say the Sons of Liberty chipped in. Others credit Hancock with supplying the goods. In any case, Adams was now properly outfitted to go to Congress and meet with leaders such as Thomas Jefferson, Patrick Henry, and George Washington.

In the eighteenth century, Philadelphia was considered the most intellectually exciting city in

61

Philadelphia was the cultural center of America before and during the Revolution.

America. Benjamin Franklin—another delegate to the Congress—had founded the Philosophical Society there. This organization encouraged scientific experiments, inventions, new medical methods, plant cultivation, and the arts. Philadelphia's streets were lined with bookstores and print shops. Seven newspapers and countless magazines were published regularly. Finally, because it was located halfway between the two most powerful colonies— Massachusetts and Virginia—it was a convenient meeting point.

Adams arrived in Philadelphia with the other delegates in August. At the first session of the

Continental Congress, which opened on September 5, 1774, men from 12 of the 13 colonies filled Carpenter's Hall. Only Georgia did not sent representatives. Many delegates were people with whom Adams had corresponded over the years.

On September 17, Adams introduced the Suffolk Resolves to Congress. This document described the situation in Massachusetts and called for the colonists to boycott British goods and refuse to pay taxes. When the document was read, the hall burst into cheers, and many delegates vowed to support Massachusetts.

Not everyone supported Adams's position. One of his opponents, Joseph Galloway, called the resolves "inflammatory" and said they "contained a complete declaration of war against Great Britain." Few delegates, no matter how dissatisfied they were with the policies of the British government, were ready to embrace the prospect of war. The resolves did not pass, but Adams's position—that the colonies break from England completely—was now clear.

One delegate who agreed with Adams was Patrick Henry of Virginia. Henry spoke movingly to

Patrick Henry was known as "The Samuel Adams of Virginia."

63

try to bind the delegates in a common cause. "I am not a Virginian," he proclaimed, "but an American!"

As the session continued, the Congress agreed to send a formal appeal to the king to moderate his policies. Henry composed a draft of the complaint, but his words were so forceful that delegates who felt strong ties to England replaced him with another writer who was less extreme.

The new committee, in Adams's view, understated the colonists' indignation because they humbly appealed to the king's "wisdom, goodness, and concern for his people's welfare." His cousin John Adams believed the address would be treated as so much "waste paper" by the king.

Before the Congress adjourned, the representatives agreed that the colonies should cease almost all trade with Britain. They renewed a call to boycott incoming English goods and to halt the export of American products to England. The delegates also instructed the colonies to arm and drill their militias. The Congress decided it would assemble again the following spring in Philadelphia.

"Put Them to the Sword!"

When Adams and the rest of the Massachusetts delegation returned to Boston in late 1774, they were greeted with churchbells and cheers from the members of the Liberty Party and other antiroyal sympathizers. The Loyalist Tories urged royal troops to kill Adams, Hancock, and several associates.

They drew up a list of names and instructed redcoats to "put the above persons to the sword" at the first hint of rebellion.

As 1775 began, a buildup toward war became evident in and around Boston. Patriot militia, who called themselves minutemen because they could be ready to fight at a moment's notice, drilled in towns around Boston. More British troops poured into the city. Refugees fled Boston, which suffered a food shortage caused by the trade embargo. Redcoats took over homes and openly harassed any citizens who expressed rebellious sentiments.

Throughout late winter and into early spring of 1775, each side warily noted the other's activities. Whenever Patriots held meetings in the city, soldiers watched them and waited for a chance to arrest Adams and "his willing and ready tool" Hancock. On the Patriot side, groups throughout Massachusetts observed the movements of British soldiers closely. One such group, Paul Revere's voluntary association of Boston mechanics,

Paul Revere was a respected Boston craftsman and Patriot.

65

held secret meetings in Concord. Revere later wrote:

> "I was one of upwards of thirty who formed ourselves into a committee for the purpose of watching the movements of the British soldiers, and gaining every intelligence of the movements of the Tories."

On April 14, orders arrived for Gage aboard the H.M.S. *Nautilus*. Dated January 27, 1775, the orders instructed Gage to act immediately against "proceedings that amount to actual revolt." He was ordered to seize the leaders of the colonial protests—men such as Samuel Adams and John Hancock. In addition, Gage was ordered to take all weapons and military supplies away from the rebels.

It was apparent from the orders that Parliament had reached the limits of its patience with its American subjects. The earl of Dartmouth, a member of the House of Lords, stated, "It is the opinion of the King's servants, in which His Majesty concurs, that the first and essential step to be taken towards re-establishing Government, would be to arrest and imprison the principal actors and abettors of the Provincial Congress whose proceedings appear... to be acts of treason."

The British government believed that it would not be difficult to crush a rebellion in the American colonies. British troops had ended revolts in other parts of the British Empire, such as Ireland and

66

Scotland. The main mission of the British army, in fact, was to destroy rebellious elements, and British soldiers were well trained to carry out the task. Many experienced soldiers stationed in Boston had also served in Ireland and Scotland. Others had helped keep the peace and stop riots in England itself.

In response to his orders, Gage drew up plans to march to Concord and capture the supplies that were believed to be stored there. He laid out part of the route by water so his men would have fewer miles to march. Gage also believed he had an excellent chance to capture two rebel ringleaders— Hancock and Adams. Spies had reported that the two men had left Boston to attend a meeting and were probably somewhere in Lexington.

The British government had already criticized Gage severely on several occasions for not arresting Hancock and Adams. Now he could end the criticism if he destroyed the weapons at Concord and captured the two rebel leaders in one mission.

On March 22, just before the Second Continental Congress was due to meet in Philadelphia, Adams had left Boston to attend the Provincial Congress— a meeting of Massachusetts Patriots—in Concord. Afterward, his advisers said he and Hancock would be safer in Lexington than they would be if they returned to Boston. The two men decided to lodge with Reverend Jonas Clarke, his wife, and their 10 children until it was time to attend the congress in Philadelphia.

Just after midnight on April 19, the crowded household was awakened by shouts at the door. The events over the next several hours brought the colonies into the American Revolution.

From Concord to Congress

Adams and Hancock watched the battle on Lexington Green from a distance, and were soon spirited away to a safe house. After the battle, British major Pitcairn's men joined another force and marched west toward Concord, where they knew the Patriots' ammunition was stored. By that point, the alarm had spread quickly to neighboring towns. When the British arrived just outside of Concord at about 7 o'clock in the morning, more than 400 militiamen awaited them.

As the British marched into Concord, they were divided into three groups. Three companies of British infantry crossed the North Bridge past Punkatasset Hill toward the farm of James Barrett, the militia commander. Three other companies were posted at the bridge to keep watch on rebel movements. A third group of redcoats was ordered to search buildings in the center of town for weapons and gunpowder.

After they searched several buildings and found nothing, the frustrated redcoats in the third unit set fire to the courthouse and the blacksmith shop. The Patriots, who had assembled on Punkatasset Hill, saw the smoke. They asked Barrett whether they should allow the British to destroy the village.

Barrett ordered his men to advance, but told them not to shoot unless they were fired upon.

About 400 militiamen started down the hill toward the British soldiers at the North Bridge. The British opened fire. The first British volley was poorly aimed and missed its targets. The Americans who returned the fire killed 12 soldiers—including four officers. The heavy fire forced the British units to retreat across the bridge.

Now that Americans held the North Bridge, they had cut off the British companies that had marched to Barrett's farm. In the confusion of battle, however, some of the Patriots returned to their positions on the ridge, while others attempted to cross the bridge and attend to the fire in the village. This group scattered when the British troops who had gone toward Barrett's farm raced back to scene, drawn by the sounds of battle. Thus the redcoats were able to cross the bridge and rejoin their comrades.

By the time the troops were reunited, British officers had sent a message to Gage asking for reinforcements. The officers delayed any further action until more British soldiers arrived. By noon, when reinforcements had failed to arrive, the order was given to march back to Lexington empty handed.

At Merriam's Corner, along the road, the British fired at a group of militiamen. The militiamen did not hesitate to return the fire. From that moment

★

In the spring of 1775, Scottish immigrant John Paul Jones left Virginia for Philadelphia to seek a commission in the newly formed Continental navy.

★

on, the road to Lexington became a route of revenge for the militiamen.

Their fifes and drums silent, the British soldiers faced constant attack. American snipers, hiding behind trees, rocks, and any cover available, picked off soldiers as they marched. Other militiamen

The retreat from Concord was a bloody defeat for the British.

ambushed the soldiers at every opportunity. They fired from behind houses, barns, and walls. As the British continued to march, they left their dead and wounded behind along the road.

There was no letup on the fire. One company of militia replaced another and another along the way. As the British soldiers neared Lexington, their discipline and courage broke down. The redcoats panicked and began to run from the musket balls that whistled from every direction.

When fleeing redcoats came dangerously close to the home where Adams and Hancock were hidden, the two men rode into a swamp and waited until the danger passed. After they witnessed the battle, Adams and Hancock began the long journey south to Philadelphia. There, they were determined to help create a new government.

Chapter 5

THE FATHER
OF FREEDOM

T he mood of the country was far different when
the Continental Congress met for the second time
in May 1775 than it had been during the first
session. Every colony had quickly heard of the
battles at Lexington and Concord. Now the
colonists knew that the British would use open
warfare to enforce their domination of America.
The people looked to the members of the Congress,
whom they had come to respect, to set the course.

OPPOSITE: John Hancock wrote his name prominently on the
Declaration of Independence.

73

The task of the Second Continental Congress was to consider "the dangerous and critical situation" in America. Lexington and Concord had convinced most delegates that war was necessary, but they disagreed on what they hoped to accomplish by going to war. While a growing number of delegates, like Adams, were ready to fight for complete independence, many hoped to reconcile their differences and remain subjects of the Crown.

For their part, the British were unwilling to address the colonies' grievances or relax royal policies. King George III denounced the "association" of colonial governments, and declared they were "in rebellion." In Boston that June, Gage issued an edict that offered to give the king's "most gracious pardon to all persons who shall forthwith lay down their arms"—all except Adams or Hancock. Their role as visible and vocal leaders of the Patriots could not go unpunished.

The delegates in Philadelphia drew up a new petition to the king that once again outlined their grievances, but also humbly sought compromise. Adams's cousin John hated the document, and compared it to holding a sword in one hand and an olive branch (a symbol of peace) in the other. Such a position, he believed, would result in a return to tyranny because it made the colonists appear uncertain of their objective.

While they waited for a royal response, the delegates' next order of business was to elect a new president of the congress. Both Adamses campaigned for Hancock. He was popular at home in the North, and as a wealthy merchant, found favor with the southern plantation owners as well. On May 24, Hancock was elected to preside over the congress.

John Adams, Samuel's younger cousin, was a successful Boston lawyer.

In Parliament, the British prime minister, Lord Frederick North, responded to the petition from America with an offer of compromise. Britain would withdraw taxes used to pay for royal appointees and troops in the colonies, North said, but it would keep the right to levy taxes to regulate colonial commerce.

Those delegates unwilling to fully break from England wanted to accept the offer. Adams and other independence-minded delegates saw North's plan as an attempt to divide Americans. He was angered further when North sent a letter in which he threatened to use the "whole force of the Kingdom ... to reduce the rebellious ... Colonies" if they did not accept the proposal.

By that time, hostilities in the North had resumed. Gage declared martial law in Boston. Laws would be enforced by the military instead of the city's judicial system. All citizens were ordered to lay down their arms or be considered traitors.

More soldiers arrived from England, as did two more generals.

Boston sought aid from the Continental Congress to defend itself, and the house instructed companies of riflemen to march to Boston from the other colonies. On June 14, the delegates created an official Continental army "for the defense of American Liberty." John Adams nominated the modest but capable George Washington from Virginia to lead the army. Samuel Adams seconded the nomination.

Washington had commanded troops, with varying degrees of success, during the French and Indian War. After the war, he was elected to the Virginia House of Burgesses, the colony's legislature. Throughout the 1760s, England's tax policies had infuriated him. In one speech to the house, he said that Parliament "hath no more right to put their hands into my pocket, without my consent, than I have to put my hands into yours for money."

Though Washington was uncertain that complete independence from England was wise, he was deeply angered by the British treatment of Boston colonists. In short, he was ready to use armed force to protect the colonists' rights if necessary. Washington left Philadelphia for Boston on June 15, 1775.

The Battle of Bunker Hill

Gage's forces in Boston now numbered close to 6,000 and they controlled the city. Patriot militias

Inexperienced Patriots faced crack British troops on Breed's Hill, near Boston.

surrounded Boston with men from Connecticut, Rhode Island, New Hampshire, Pennsylvania, Maryland, and Virginia. These units had set out for Massachusetts after they learned of the battles at Lexington and Concord. They were eager to fight, but they were not well trained.

General Samuel Ward was in charge of the Massachusetts militia. He was as zealous as Adams in his belief in colonists' rights. Ward ordered his second in command, Colonel William Prescott, to fortify Bunker Hill and Breed's Hill in Charlestown, across Boston Harbor. They dug all night on June 16 to entrench themselves on Charlestown peninsula. The next day, they were joined by Israel Putnam's men from Connecticut.

Samuel Adams

On the morning of June 17, British warships attacked the new fortifications. Nearly 2,300 redcoats—more than twice the Patriots' force—rowed ashore and began to assault the hills. The Patriots fought back against two assaults. Because they were dreadfully short on gunpowder, Prescott ordered his men not to fire at the redcoats until they could "see the whites of their eyes." When the redcoats made a third approach on the hills, the Patriots ran out of ammunition. They were reduced to fighting British regulars with their fists.

When the battle was over, 1,054 redcoats had been killed or wounded, including Pitcairn, who had led the fight at Lexington. The Americans had far fewer casualties, about 400. Among the losses was Dr. Joseph Warren, one of Adams's closest associates. Adams mourned the loss of his compatriot, but the battle raised his hopes for an eventual victory. Although the Patriots had been defeated, they had shown the British that Americans would fight to the death for their rights. Adams called the battle "a triumph indeed!"

Toward Independence

June 17 was a decisive day on the road to revolution. In Britain, George III now considered the conflict in America a foreign war and not an internal affair. The other colonies realized that the Crown meant to exert its will by force. Still, a majority of citizens and representatives had not decided whether the colonies should split completely with England.

With unfailing energy, 53-year-old Adams continued to write many more letters and essays to try to convince people that it was necessary to declare independence. Another writer, who borrowed ideas from Adams, became the driving force that helped to turn the tide. His name was Thomas Paine.

In January 1776, Paine published a pamphlet called *Common Sense*, which laid out in plain language the reasons why the colonies should sever ties from Britain. "Now is the seedtime of continental union, faith, and honor," he wrote. England was not the "motherland," but a "monster," he said, and independence was a person's natural right. A record half million copies of Paine's booklet were sold, and countless Americans were persuaded of their right to be free.

In February, Parliament issued a prohibition on trade with the colonies. George III hired German mercenaries,

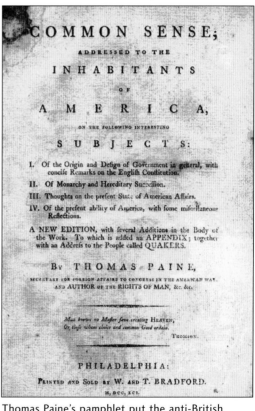

Thomas Paine's pamphlet put the anti-British feelings of many colonists into words.

Paine and Adams

★ ★ ★ ★ ★

Although Thomas Paine was born in 1737 (15 years after Samuel Adams) and lived in England until 1774, Paine and Adams shared a number of similarities. Both men's fathers were working men—Adams's a brewer and Paine's a staymaker (a maker of women's corsets). Paine, like Adams, grew up surrounded by working people. Both fathers rejected the official state religion of England, the Anglican Church. The elder Adams was a devout Congregationalist, and Paine's father was a devout Quaker. Thomas Paine, like Adams, absorbed his father's beliefs as he grew. Many of those beliefs centered on a distrust of the monarchy and the enormous advantage held by the wealthy in British society. Unlike Adams, Paine left school at age 13. He was self-taught and well-read, but, like Adams, he was not certain what he wanted to do with his life. After he rejected the life of a staymaker, Paine became a tax

Thomas Paine and Adams had similar beliefs about government.

called Hessians, to join the ranks of his redcoats. A giant armada of ships, filled with these reinforcements, headed toward the colonies.

80

collector. Like Adams, Paine felt uncomfortable collecting taxes from working people and eventually was fired from his job for incompetence. In his early thirties, Paine belonged to a club called the Headstrong Club, which met at a local tavern to debate political issues in much the same manner as Adams's Whipping-Post Club did.

Paine left England for Philadelphia in 1774 with a letter of recommendation from Benjamin Franklin, whom he had befriended in London. He quickly found a job as a magazine editor, and in one of his first pieces, he criticized Americans for permitting slavery, a practice that Adams also hated.

Paine and Adams met during the Second Continental Congress and immediately realized that they agreed the colonies should separate from England. Delegates in Congress discussed the pros and cons of such action, but unlike Adams and Paine, most still hoped to find a way to make amends with England.

For Paine, like Adams, compromise was out of the question. How could a gigantic, prosperous, and energetic continent be ruled by a small island thousands of miles away? he wondered. The king of that island had also used force against his own subjects. That alone seemed to make a complete break necessary.

As soon as he read *Common Sense*, Adams realized its importance. He wrote that Paine's work "unquestionably awakened the public mind, and led the people loudly to call for a declaration of our national independence." Although the two men saw little of each other after the first years of the Revolution, they corresponded until Adams's death in 1802. Paine died seven years later.

The Continental Congress now began to receive urgent instructions from their home legislatures to move toward self-rule. On June 7, 1776, Henry

Lee of Virginia made a formal motion to declare America a union of independent states. Finally, Adams's vision was at hand. "The child Independence is now struggling for birth," he said. If America was to be truly separate, however, the decision had to be unanimous, he believed. The colonies had to present a united front against the mightiest power on earth. Before the vote on independence was taken, Adams had to win more delegates over to his side.

While fellow delegate and respected writer Thomas Jefferson prepared a draft of a declaration of independence, Adams argued masterfully with those who were undecided. He would stand straight and gaze right at the person with his dark blue eyes. His words were strong and deeply felt as he questioned, explained, and appealed to reason.

Finally, on July 2, a vote was taken in the Continental Congress. No colony wanted to stand in the way of the voice of the country. Although a few men abstained, each delegation in turn voted for independence. Adams praised this vote as "the decisive measure."

The Declaration Document

On July 4, the president of the Congress, John Hancock, affixed his bold signature to the document called the Declaration of Independence. He wrote in such a large hand, he said, so George III "can read my name without spectacles and may double his reward on my head!" With the document signed, delegate Benjamin Franklin humorously encouraged all the delegates to "hang together," lest they all "hang separately." Adams signed "Saml Adams," using a short form of his name.

The declaration was circulated throughout the colonies and read aloud to cheering crowds from statehouse steps and balconies. In Philadelphia on July 8, the giant Liberty Bell was rung to celebrate the document.

True to his modest personality, Adams did not take credit for his role in the movement to independence, but placed it elsewhere. "The hand of Heaven appears to have led us on," he proclaimed in a speech before the Continental Congress. The address was delivered on August 1, 1776, one day before the delegates signed the formal parchment copy of the Declaration of Independence.

★

On August 1, 1776, the Marine Committee of the Continental Congress placed John Paul Jones in command of the American warship *Providence*.

★

Celebrations had wound down, and the country now faced an enormous challenge. The British army had more than 30,000 professional soldiers and the most powerful navy in the world. The Americans had at most 20,000 men, who were barely trained, poorly outfitted, and badly equipped. There was little naval support.

Many of the delegates to the Continental Congress were exhausted from several long, hot months of debate and deliberation. Of the men from Massachusetts alone, Hancock suffered from gout, or inflamed joints; John Adams had nervous

"He Who Has Most Zeal"

★ ★ ★ ★ ★

During the early years of the Revolution, there was no solid agreement among representatives to the Continental Congress about whether the colonies should declare independence. Even after the Declaration of Independence was approved, some colonists were reluctant to take such a momentous step. It was during this time that Adams, at age 54, one of the oldest representatives, spoke out with unflagging zeal about the cause of liberty. On August 1, 1776, less than a month after the Declaration of Independence was approved, Adams took the floor and delivered a lengthy speech to his fellow representatives to convince them that the path the new nation had chosen was right. Among his words that day were these:

> *Men who content themselves with the semblance of truth, and a display of words, talk much of our obligations to Great Britain for protection. Had she a single eye to our advantage? . . . She has treated us as beasts of burthen. Did the protection we received annul our rights as men and lay us under an obligation of being miserable? Who among you, my countrymen, that is a father, would*

tremors, inflamed eyes, and was on the verge of collapse; and Samuel Adams was described as "completely worn out."

84

claim authority to make your child a slave because you had nourished him in infancy?

    This day presents the world with the . . . spectacle . . . of freemen deliberately and voluntarily forming themselves into a society for their common defense and common happiness. . . . Here no man proclaims his birth or wealth as a title to honorable distinction. . . . He who has most zeal . . . let him be the servant of the public.

    For my own part, I ask no greater blessing than to share with you the common danger and common glory. . . . If I have a wish dearer to my soul [it is] that these American States may never cease to be free and independent.

The Second Continental Congress met in Carpenter's Hall, in Philadelphia.

    Still, Adams knew that someone would have to serve in the government. To declare independence was one thing. To secure it was quite another.

85

Samuel Adams

Chapter 6

A CHAMPION
OF RIGHTS

Although Adams was not a soldier and was a good deal older than many of the founders of the new nation, he possessed more energy and passion for the cause of freedom than most Patriots. He deeply believed that Americans could build a better world. "As long as the people are virtuous," he said, "they cannot be subdued. This will be their great security."

OPPOSITE: French troops landed in Rhode Island in 1780 to aid the Continental army.

Throughout much of his adult life, Adams's skill at agitation had turned a city, a colony, and a nation against British oppression. Now he summoned the energy to continue the battle and lead the nation to liberty.

The Toll of War

For a delegate to summon energy was one matter. To assemble supplies and food for the men who fought was a much more difficult problem to address. For the men on the battlefield, the war was nasty and brutal. Food, clothing, weapons, and medicine were scarce. The Continental Congress's War Office was charged with raising funds for the army, but there was little colonial currency. Most of the funds used to pay for the war were borrowed from foreign governments. Yet those loans did little to support a war that dragged on for more than six years.

American soldiers received supplies from Congress's War Office thanks to work done by Adams.

88

Though Adams did not serve in the War Office, he worked with it to provide Washington with troops and supplies. Other delegates even began to call Adams "The General" because of his efforts on behalf of the troops. Adams's concern about the army's hardships led him to express his resentment of Hancock's personal lifestyle, which continued to be lavish. Hancock replied that he had contributed far more money to the independence movement than Adams had ever made, so he had no right to criticize.

The stress of the time caused the two men to argue, and a bitterness developed between them. As the events in the first year of the war grew more discouraging, Hancock started a false rumor that Adams wanted Washington to be replaced with a more effective general. Because Washington was held in such high regard, the rumor damaged Adams's reputation among many colonists.

Articles of Confederation

During the first two years of war, Adams worked chiefly with representatives from the 13 new states to establish procedures for the new government. They issued Articles of War, which detailed the operation, ranks, and pay of the forces. They also issued Continental currency. They debated and decided a variety of issues, including how the representatives should vote during sessions, deal with spies, and define boundaries. Their biggest challenge was to establish a plan of government for

89

Continental money was of little value to most colonists.

the United States.

Adams served on the committee that wrote a document for the new union of independent states. The Articles of Confederation, as it was called, was drafted in 1777. This first attempt to form a national constitution was the forerunner of the U.S. Constitution.

Adams, like many delegates, was opposed to a strong central government. His experiences with Parliament convinced him that the new states should be at least as powerful individually as a central, or federal, government. He and the other delegates put their conviction into the Articles of Confederation.

Under the articles, the states retained "sovereignty, freedom and independence." The national legislature, called Congress, was given the responsibility for foreign affairs. It had the power to declare war and peace and to maintain an army and navy. The legislature had no power to collect taxes, regulate commerce between the states, or enforce laws.

While Adams spent much of the war working out the details of the government, his most important contribution was to strengthen the spirit of liberty. When the redcoats approached Philadelphia in September 1777, Congress fled west to York.

90

There, Adams gave a speech to lift morale among the discouraged delegates:

"Gentlemen, Your spirits appear oppressed with the weight of the public calamities. . . . Our affairs, it is said, are desperate! . . . [But] If we wear long faces, long faces will become fashionable. The eyes of the people are upon us. . . . Our burdens, though grievous, can be borne. Our losses, though great, can be retrieved. Through the darkness which shrouds our prospects, the ark of safety is visible. Despondency becomes not the dignity of our cause. . . . Let us awake then, and evince a . . . spirit that shall inspire the people with confidence . . . a spirit that will encourage them to persevere in this glorious struggle, until their rights and liberties shall be established on a rock!"

Many delegates, who by that time feared that the Revolution was already lost, thought Adams had lost his mind. They were even more convinced when he concluded his speech with the words, "Good tidings will soon arrive!"

Coincidentally, less than three weeks after that speech, the Americans won their biggest victory in the war. At Saratoga, New York, more than 5,000 British troops were forced to surrender on October 17. This victory convinced France that the young United States was indeed an ally worthy of support. An alliance agreement was signed the next spring.

The following year, France sent troops, ships, and supplies to the Continental army.

By April 1781, when the Articles of Confederation were at last ratified by the states, Adams felt that his work in Congress was finished. At 58 years of age, he was fatigued and "wished for the Sweets of Retirement."

Just six months later, on October 19, the American and French troops, assisted by the French navy, trapped British general Charles Cornwallis and 8,000 troops at Yorktown, Virginia, and forced their surrender. The fighting was over.

Cornwallis surrendered to Washington at Yorktown, Virginia, after more than a week of artillery bombardment from American and French forces.

Man of Massachusetts

When Adams returned to his home state in April 1781, he had been away for almost six years. His reunion with his wife Betsy was joyous. Hannah, his daughter, was now 25 years old and engaged to be married. Not so joyous was the situation with Adams's son, Samuel. The young doctor, who had studied under Joseph Warren, suffered from tuberculosis he contracted while in the army.

The reunited family lived in a large yellow house on Winter Street that was rented to them by the state government. They were never able to return to Adams's father's home on Purchase Street, which had been ruined beyond repair by the redcoats before they abandoned Boston in 1776.

Despite his desire to retire, Adams continued to serve in the state legislature for a number of years. There, with John Adams and another delegate, James Bowdoin, he helped to draft the Massachusetts Constitution.

In 1783, the treaty that formally ended the Revolution was signed in Paris. The country was in high spirits, but Adams was out of fashion again. He ran for the office of lieutenant governor, but lost.

Adams continued to work on causes that were important to him. He led the fight against slavery in Massachusetts, and the state abolished it in 1783. He visited schools and worked to improve the educational system so that all children would have an equal right to learn and attend school.

93

A New Constitution

Throughout much of the 1780s, the United States was governed by the Articles of Confederation, which Adams had helped to write. By 1787, lawmakers had serious doubts about the document. The federal government had amassed large bills it could not pay because it had no power to tax the states. There was no federal court system and no executive branch. Congress had no permanent building.

Individual states had become more powerful than the federal government. Some people, including Adams, Thomas Jefferson, and Patrick Henry, believed that was appropriate. After they had rid America of oppressors who taxed from outside the country, they did not want to encourage tyranny from within. These men felt the Articles of Confederation could be revised and improved but should not be wholly replaced. Federalists, on the other hand, supported

The Treaty of Paris, signed by John Adams and other Americans, officially ended the Revolution.

Washington was a strong presence at the 1787 Constitutional Convention although he said little.

a strong central government. They wanted to create an entirely new framework, a new constitution that would reorganize the government. John Adams was one of these men. John Hancock, now governor of Massachusetts, was undecided.

In early 1787, the Confederation Congress supported a plan to hold a convention for the purpose of revising the Articles of Confederation. The convention was held at Independence Hall in Philadelphia in May. Many former delegates, including Adams and Henry, refused to take part in the creation of what they viewed as an overly powerful federal government.

In the end, a new U.S. Constitution was written at the convention. In order to go into effect, it had to be ratified by at least two-thirds of the states. Each state held a convention to decide whether it would accept or reject the new document.

Both Adams and Hancock were chosen to attend the Massachusetts meeting. After they had feuded for years, they had found themselves on the same side in opposition to the ratification. This presented an opportunity for them to finally speak to one another again, and their friendship was renewed.

Debate at the Massachusetts convention went on for days. Some did not like the power that was invested in the presidency of the United States. Others thought elections were called too frequently. The discussions were suddenly interrupted when Adams's son died of tuberculosis.

A few days after the funeral, Adams met with Paul Revere and some working men—dockworkers, mechanics, and farmers. These former Sons of Liberty told Adams they supported the new Constitution. Because the Sons had been an important force during the Revolution, Adams listened. So did Hancock. Though they still did not totally agree with the document, they began to see it in a new light.

The problem with the Constitution, both men agreed, was that it did not clearly state a citizen's civil rights. Unless a list of such rights was included, they feared, the federal government might overpower the people. They wanted amendments to the Constitution that would protect certain rights: Citizens would be free to worship whatever religion they chose, assemble and petition the government, speak freely without punishment, keep and bear arms, and refuse lawless quartering of soldiers. They would be protected against unlawful search and seizure, and have the right to a speedy public trial by jury.

Adams proposed these amendments to the Constitution before the Massachusetts convention. When the vote was taken in 1788, Massachusetts ratified the Constitution by a narrow margin. Adams's sentiments were shared by many other Americans, including James Madison and George Mason of Virginia, who drafted the Bill of Rights that assured all Americans of their basic liberties.

★

In June 1788, John and Abigail Adams returned to Massachusetts after John had served for three years as a U.S. diplomat in London.

★

Even Federalists came to agree that the Bill of Rights was necessary. Once they were drafted, other states ratified the document, and by 1790, all 13 states had approved the new Constitution. Without the Bill of Rights, however, and without Adams's insistence on its inclusion, the U.S. Constitution may never have been ratified. Many people consider this contribution to the Constitution one of Adams's greatest services to the country.

Governor of His State

By 1789, Hancock and Adams were both getting on in years. Hancock, 53, had suffered for years from gout, and was so ill that he often could not walk. Adams, now 67, trembled so severely from a nerve disorder that he had to have other people write his papers for him.

97

Although they were not in the best of health, their friendship had been renewed during the debate over ratification of the U.S. Constitution. Hancock and Adams ran together in 1789 for governor and lieutenant governor of Massachusetts. They were elected to the highest state positions and served together for four years.

In 1793, Hancock died, and a large state funeral was held for him. Adams took part in the procession, which passed the spot where the old Liberty Tree had stood before the British had chopped it down.

Upon Hancock's death, Adams assumed the role of governor at the age of 71. The next spring, he ran on his own and was easily re-elected, as he was again in 1795 and 1796. Adams was the oldest governor ever to have served the state of Massachusetts.

In 1796, supporters urged Adams to run for president, but he was not interested. At 74, he would not even seek re-election to the governorship. "The infirmities of age render me an unfit person," he said. Adams received 11 electoral votes for president anyway.

The chief executive position went to John Adams. Samuel Adams did not always agree with his cousin politically, but he wrote to him on his inauguration, saying, "I congratulate you as the first citizen of the United States—I may add the world. I am, my dear sir... your old and unvaried friend."

Samuel Adams loved strolling along the docks of Boston Harbor throughout his long life.

Final Days

In his seventies, Adams still strolled about the streets of Boston—he preferred not to use a carriage. He visited the dockworkers and taverngoers to listen to their ideas. His great-grandson William Wells described his appearance:

"He wore a tie-wig, cocked hat, buckled shoes, knee breeches, and a red cloak, and held himself very erect, with the ease and address of a polite gentleman. On stopping to speak with any person in the street his salutation was formal yet cordial. His gestures were animated, and in conversation there was a slight tremulous motion of the head.... The eyebrows were

heavy, almost to bushiness, and contrasted remarkably with the clear forehead, which ... had but few wrinkles. The face had a benign but careworn expression, blended with a native dignity (some have said majesty) of countenance which never failed to impress strangers."

By the time he turned 80, in 1802, Adams could not walk much farther than his own home and garden. He eventually became bedridden, and on October 2, 1803, he died, with Betsy by his side.

Adams had requested to be buried in a simple wooden coffin, without show or parade. The people of Massachusetts, however, felt he deserved to be treated with honor, like a respected statesman. They accompanied his coffin through the streets of Boston to the Granary Burial Ground. Bells rang and cannons fired in a final salute to the man who had led them from oppression to liberty.

Samuel Adams, Patriot and revolutionary, spent much of his life envisioning a country founded on virtue, freedom, and equality. With unflagging energy, he brought that vision to life and kept it focused when it threatened to fade. George Clymer, a fellow delegate to the Continental Congress, said of Adams, "All good Americans should erect a statue to him in their hearts."

Glossary

activism organized political action to protest policy

boycott an organized refusal to buy certain goods

confederation a union, such as the United States

Congregational a Protestant sect that governs itself

Continental Congress the first congress of united colonies

Crown the royal British monarch and government

Federalist a supporter of strong central government

House of Burgesses a legislative body representing boroughs or towns in Virginia

effigy an image of a person hung or burned in protest

Loyalist a person who supports the ruling government

militia a body of citizens called out to fight in emergencies

Navigation Acts Laws passed by the British Parliament in the late 1600s that controlled trade between England and the colonies

Parliament the ruling legislature of Great Britain

Patriots colonists who supported and fought for their country

propaganda materials sent out by zealous members of a movement representing their views and principles

radical a person who holds extreme or contrary views

redcoats British soldiers, who wore red jacketed uniforms

repeal to withdraw officially, as a law or an act

Sons of Liberty Colonists who protested British oppression

treason a violation of allegiance to one's country

tyranny the abuse of power by a tyrant

zeal ardently devotion; passionate support

For More Information

Books

Fowler, Lillian, et al. *Samuel Adams: Radical Puritan*. Boston: AddisonWesley, 1997.

Fradin, Dennis. *Samuel Adams: The Father of American Independence*. New York: Clarion Books, 1998.

Jones, Veda Boyd, et al. *Samuel Adams: Patriot*. Pennsylvania: Chelsea House, 2001.

McDowell, Bart. *The Revolutionary War*. Washington, D.C.: National Geographic Society, 1967.

Miller, Lillian B., et al. *"The Dye Is Now Cast": The Road to American Independence, 1775–1776*. Washington, D.C.: Smithsonian Institution Press, 1975.

Richardson, Fayette. *Sam Adams: The Boy Who Became Father of the American Revolution*. New York: Crown Publishers, 1975.

Web Sites

Virtual American Biographies
http://www.virtualology.com/samueladams
This site includes detailed but easy-to-read information on the man, his associates, and his influence.

Wake Forest University: Portrait of a People Series
http://www.wfu.edu/Academic-departments/History/
newnation/adams/Sam.htm
This site is organized into informative sections—introduction, personal, people, propaganda, principles, events—and includes a time line and bibliography.

Index

104